SEE ME
HEAR ME
KNOW ME

from

The Heart of A Caregiver

PROMISE
Publishing House

~{ **JOURNAL** }~

EVELYN JOHNSON-TAYLOR Ph.D.
CONTRIBUTING AUTHOR: SCOTT B. TAYLOR

See Me Hear Me Know Me {JOURNAL}

See Me Hear Me Know Me – *The Heart of a Caregiver* {JOURNAL}
Copyright © 2017 Evelyn Johnson-Taylor and Scott B. Taylor

All rights reserved. No part of this publication may be reproduced, stored in a retrieval system, or transmitted in any form or by any means, electronic, mechanical, digital, photocopy, recording, or any other except for brief quotation in printed reviews, without the prior permission of the publisher.

Unless otherwise indicated, all Scripture quotations are taken from THE HOLY BIBLE, NEW INTERNATIONAL VERSION®, NIV® Copyright © 1973, 1978, 1984, 2011 by Biblica, Inc.™ Used by permission of Zondervan. All rights reserved worldwide. www.zondervan.com. Scriptures marked KJV are taken from the King James Version of the Bible. The KJV is public domain in the United States.

Please note that Promise Publishing House will capitalize all pronouns that refer to the Father, Son, and Holy Spirit. Note that the name satan and related names are not capitalized. We choose not to give him the same acknowledgement, even to the point of violating the rules of grammar.

Published by:

PROMISE PUBLISHING HOUSE
PO Box 46753, Tampa FL 33646 | www.promisepublishinghouse.com

FIRST EDITION ~ JOURNAL

Library of Congress Control Number: 2016921555

Written by: Evelyn Johnson-Taylor Ph.D. and Scott B. Taylor

Cover and Formatting by: Eli Blyden

ISBN: 978-0-9908338-6-4

Category: Motivational/Inspirational/Christian

For Worldwide Distribution

Printed in the U.S. A.

Reasons to Journal

FOCUS

*

CLARITY

*

CALMING

*

GRATITUDE

*

MEMORIES

*

SELF-EVALUATION

*

PERSONAL GROWTH

See Me Hear Me Know Me {JOURNAL}

Table of Contents

Reasons to Journal III
Let's Journal VII

JOURNAL YOUR THOUGHTS
  Caregiver's Grieving Heart 3
  Heart of Contentment 7
  Heart of Faith 11
  Forgiving Heart 15
  Heart to do Good 19
  Hopeful Heart 23
  Kind and Loving Heart 27
  Lonely Heart 31
  Heart of Patience 35
  Peaceful Heart 39
  Quiet my Heart 43
  Thankful Heart 47

See Me Hear Me Know Me **{JOURNAL}**

Let's Journal

For many years I have enjoyed the benefits of journaling. Writing is cathartic. When I write, it helps to bring clarity and understanding to my thoughts. It allows me to release negative emotions and reevaluate how I should proceed.

Putting my thoughts on paper allows me to trace my growth and development. As one matures chronologically, hopefully there is a measure of mental maturity that is observed. Reading my journals permits me to see just how far I have come or the lack thereof in some cases. Nevertheless, it is a time for me to see what I need to adjust, discontinue, or begin.

Journaling allows me to track God. I am encouraged when I see how God has answered previous prayers. When I read in my journal of situations that appeared difficult, I can also read how God manifested His favor. That is the moment I am assured that He will do it again. God does not change and His same power is available each day to those who trust and believe.

We like to think our memory retention is great, but it may surprise us to know how much we forget. Life is busy and many are moving very fast trying to maintain. The brain retains a limited amount of what is observed and heard. Journaling is a way to keep close our treasured memories and lessons learned.

Without my journals I would not have been able to write: See Me, Hear Me, Know Me, from The Heart of a Caregiver. Many things have happened over the course of the last nine years, some of which I had forgotten. It's interesting that when we are in the middle of a crisis, we may think there's no way we can forget it even if we wanted to. One of the blessings of the mind is the ability to not remember some of the trauma related to an experience. Not remembering allows us to move forward.

As I read my journal entries I was reminded of some experiences that I want to share with my readers. It is my desire that as you read the book you will be motivated to use this accompanying journal as well for I truly believe it will be therapeutic. Journaling will allow you to release your emotions in a safe space first. After journaling if you still feel the need to talk, then go ahead and do that as well.

Each chapter of the book is covered in this journal; there are thought-provoking questions to stimulate your thought process. Feel free to add your own thoughts as you write. There may be a personal encounter that you have experienced that was not covered in the book, so write it out.

On the back cover of this journal you will see partial quotes from several individuals in how journaling has benefited them; there is a broad age range of those who contributed. To journal is rewarding for any age group, male or female. I would love to have feedback from you regarding your experience with the book and journal. My contact information is evelynjtaylor@evelynjtaylor.org.

See Me Hear Me Know Me **{JOURNAL}**

Caregiver's Grieving Heart

Matthew 5:1-3 - Now when Jesus saw the crowds, he went up on a mountainside and sat down. His disciples came to him, and he began to teach them. He said: "Blessed are the poor in spirit, for theirs is the kingdom of heaven.

* * *

What kinds of losses have you experienced during your caregiving journey? How have you dealt with the grief?

Confess any guilt you may be experiencing and write about any situations that may have caused you to feel guilt.

Pray asking God to deliver you and write out everything you believe God has placed in your heart to begin anew.

Journal your thoughts.

See Me Hear Me Know Me **{JOURNAL}**

Date_____

Caregiver's Grieving Heart

See Me Hear Me Know Me **{JOURNAL}**

Heart of Contentment

Ecclesiastes 6:9 - Better what the eye sees than the roving of the appetite. This too is meaningless, a chasing after the wind.

* * *

Identify areas in your life where you have been discontented. Pray asking God to help you to learn how to be content with your current situation.

Journal your thoughts.

See Me Hear Me Know Me **{JOURNAL}**

Date_____

Heart of Contentment

See Me Hear Me Know Me **{JOURNAL}**

Heart of Faith

James 1:6 - But when you ask, you must believe and not doubt, because the one who doubts is like a wave of the sea, blown and tossed by the wind.

* * *

Identify areas that you have exhibited a lack of faith. Why was your faith lacking in these areas?

Pray asking God to increase your faith.

Journal your thoughts.

See Me Hear Me Know Me **{JOURNAL}**

Date_____

Heart of Faith

See Me Hear Me Know Me {**JOURNAL**}

Forgiving Heart

Matthew 6:14-15 - For if you forgive other people when they sin against you, your heavenly Father will also forgive you. But if you do not forgive others their sins, your Father will not forgive your sins.

* * *

List any areas where you may be experiencing unforgiveness at this time.

Pray acknowledging all unresolved disputes and ask for forgiveness.

Journal your thoughts.

See Me Hear Me Know Me {**JOURNAL**}

Date_____

Forgiving Heart

See Me Hear Me Know Me {**JOURNAL**}

Heart to do Good

Proverbs 17:22 - A cheerful heart is good medicine, but a crushed spirit dries up the bones.

* * *

List as many reasons as you can think of to be cheerful.

Pray asking God to help you to see all the good that He has put in front of you.

Journal your thoughts

See Me Hear Me Know Me {JOURNAL}

Date_____

Heart to do Good

See Me Hear Me Know Me {**JOURNAL**}

Hopeful Heart

Romans 12:12 - Be joyful in hope, patient in affliction, faithful in prayer.

* * *

Write about your hopeless experiences.

Pray asking God to renew your hope for the future and for the plans that He has for your life.

Journal your thoughts.

See Me Hear Me Know Me **{JOURNAL}**

Date_____

Hopeful Heart

See Me Hear Me Know Me **{JOURNAL}**

Kind and Loving Heart

Colossians 3:12 - Therefore, as God's chosen people, holy and dearly loved, clothe yourselves with compassion, kindness, humility, gentleness and patience.

* * *

After an honest evaluation, in what ways can you show more kindness?

Pray asking God to help you to show kindness and to love with the love of Christ.

Journal your thoughts.

See Me Hear Me Know Me **{JOURNAL}**

Date_____

Kind and Loving Heart

See Me Hear Me Know Me {**JOURNAL**}

Lonely Heart

Isaiah 43:1-2 - (KJV) But now thus saith the Lord that created thee, O Jacob, and he that formed thee, O Israel, Fear not: for I have redeemed thee, I have called thee by thy name; thou art mine. When thou passest through the waters, I will be with thee; and through the rivers, they shall not overflow thee: when thou walkest through the fire, thou shalt not be burned; neither shall the flame kindle upon thee.

* * *

This same Word applies today, God will be with you.

Share some of your lonely moments.

Pray asking God to build strong godly relationships in your life.

Journal your thoughts.

See Me Hear Me Know Me {JOURNAL}

Date_____

Lonely Heart

See Me Hear Me Know Me {**JOURNAL**}

Heart of Patience

Romans 5:3-4 - Not only so, but we also glory in our sufferings, because we know that suffering produces perseverance; perseverance, character; and character, hope.

* * *

It can be difficult to be patient with a difficult person, even if it is someone you are caring for. Have you been impatient? Share times when you have displayed impatience.

There are so many things that we learn when we deal with long-term illness.

What has your journey as a caregiver taught you?

Reflect on the patience that God has extended toward you and pray asking for His help in extending the same grace of patience to others.

Journal your thoughts.

See Me Hear Me Know Me {**JOURNAL**}

Date_____

Heart of Patience

See Me Hear Me Know Me **{JOURNAL}**

Peaceful Heart

1 Peter 5:7 - Cast all your anxiety on him because he cares for you.

* * *

How do you deal with things that disturb your peace?

Pray asking God to grant peace in the midst of your chaos.

Journal your thoughts.

See Me Hear Me Know Me **{JOURNAL}**

Date_____

Peaceful Heart

See Me Hear Me Know Me **{JOURNAL}**

Quiet my Heart

Psalm 46:10 - He says, "Be still, and know that I am God; I will be exalted among the nations, I will be exalted in the earth."

* * *

How do you handle feelings of restlessness?

Pray asking God to help you use wisdom with the free time you have.

Journal your thoughts.

See Me Hear Me Know Me {JOURNAL}

Date_____

Quiet my Heart

See Me Hear Me Know Me {**JOURNAL**}

Thankful Heart

1 Thessalonians 5:18 - give thanks in all circumstances; for this is God's will for you in Christ Jesus.

* * *

Even though we are not thankful for all the difficulties we experience in this life, we are instructed to give thanks in all circumstances.

Write about some of the difficulties you have experienced and ways you have discovered to be thankful.

Pray a prayer of thanksgiving to God for blessing past, present and future. Ask God for His joy to flood your heart today.

Journal your thoughts.

See Me Hear Me Know Me {**JOURNAL**}

Date_____

See Me Hear Me Know Me {JOURNAL}

www.ingramcontent.com/pod-product-compliance
Lightning Source LLC
Chambersburg PA
CBHW070552300426
44113CB00011B/1878